Like A Fish Out Of Batter

Catherine Graham

Indigo Dreams Publishing

First Edition: Like A Fish Out Of Batter
First published in Great Britain in 2016 by:
Indigo Dreams Publishing Ltd
24 Forest Houses
Halwill
Beaworthy
EX21 5UU
www.indigodreams.co.uk

Catherine Graham has asserted her right under the Copyright, Designs and Patents Act 1988 to be identified as the author of this work.

ISBN 978-1-910834-30-5

British Library Cataloguing in Publication Data. A CIP record for this book can be obtained from the British Library.

Designed and typeset in Palatino Linotype by Indigo Dreams.
Cover design by Ronnie Goodyer at Indigo Dreams
Author photo ©picturesbybish (Chris Bishop)
Printed and bound in Great Britain by: 4edge Ltd
www.4edge.co.uk

Papers used by Indigo Dreams are recyclable products made from wood grown in sustainable forests following the guidance of the Forest Stewardship Council.

Dedicated to Nancy, Shirley, Kenny and Billy.

Acknowledgements

Inspired by L. S. Lowry, some of the poems in *Like A Fish Out Of Batter* bear the titles of his work. My poems give voice to the people in the paintings and my hope is that readers will seek out the pieces that have inspired me, some of which do not always spring to mind when we hear the name L. S. Lowry. Meet *Maureen* and *Ray*, characters I have created and whose story is woven through the collection. The majority of featured paintings/drawings can be viewed online at www.thelowry.com I have learnt a tremendous amount about the artist and his art from T. J. Clark and Anne M. Wagner's *Lowry and the Painting of Modern Life* (Tate Publishing, 2013) and Michael Leber and Judith Sandling's *L. S. Lowry* (Phaidon Press Ltd., 1987). A huge thank you to Jim Bennett, Managing Editor at The Poetry Kit www.poetrykit.org and members of the PK Poetry List for their invaluable support throughout my writing of this collection.

'Factory Outing' was first published in the Morning Star's, *Well Versed* (ed. Jody Porter). 'A Protest March' first appeared online at Culture Matters www.culturematters.org.uk. 'Nancy Drever' was first published in *Reach Poetry* (Indigo Dreams Publishing Ltd.).

Also by Catherine Graham:

Things I Will Put In My Mother's Pocket (IDP), 2013.
Signs (ID on Tyne Press), 2010.

CONTENTS

Factory Outing

Yachts, 1959

Red and yellow sails like flames
out on the water; the salt-sea air

so good for factory girls like me,
girls who spend their days in overalls

and daft hats; busy little workers
pounding the production line.

The two blokes in row boats look
knackered, like *me* at the end of a shift.

My ex was at the back of the bus, sat
next to her from Packaging. God she was

packed into that dress. Maybe I'll just
stand here a bit longer, imagine life

beyond that horizon, but what the hell
do I know about life beyond any horizon,

standing here looking at yachts, feeling
lost, like a fish out of batter, praying

my period will come, either that or
with the next kind wave I drown.

Girl with Bouffant Hair

My mother sits on the end of my bed,
watching me get ready to meet Ray.

'I wish you wouldn't backcomb your hair like that,
it makes you look common.'

It's never worth answering my mother,
she loves me too much to listen.

On summer days when girls played skips in the street
in nylon swimming costumes that never got wet,

I was the girl who had to keep her vest on.
Mother's notes to my teacher read like letters

to an agony aunt; the problem was never the same.
Years down the line and here we are, me (and my mother)

getting ready for my date. 'You're not going
straight out after a hot bath, our Maureen,

all them open pores; you'll catch your death!'
I put on my vest and she passes me my best white blouse,

the one with the wide collar. I check myself in the mirror:
She thinks I can't see her as she checks the length of my skirt.

Her eyes read me from head to toe
as if at an appointment with the optician.

When I put on my camel-hair coat and kitten heel shoes,
she smiles. Hoping to catch the 7 o'clock into town,

I grab my handbag and go, just in time to hear
the bus wheezing to a stop across the road.

My mother, standing on the toilet seat to reach,
pushes open the bathroom window,

'Mind you catch the last bus home!' Her voice wavers
as she closes the window and mouths my dead sister's name.

Arthur

Man in an Overcoat, 1960

I call him Arthur.
I don't know his name.

His mother
probably gave him three

plus her mother's maiden name.
She probably sang

as she pressed waves
into little Arthur's hair.

I see him every day in the park,
his little legs

running like the clappers,
chasing pigeons.

Children laugh at him
and he enjoys it.

He doesn't realise
they're making fun, not *having* it.

He'd be grand at the circus
or better still, a children's entertainer

and with those long fingers
he could give us a tune

on the old piano
if his little legs could reach the pedals.

Look at him,
still parting his hair on the side.

Wrapped
in his little brown overcoat

like a right little parcel.

Ray, Upstairs On the No.8, Waiting For It to Pull Away

Man Lying On A Wall

I don't blame you, lying down like that,
like a corpse on a slab. I mean,

it must be hard having one foot
longer than the other.

And them big fat knuckles
can only hinder a pen-pusher like you.

I see you've lit up a fag, I say lit up,
it's hard to tell from up here

but the chimneys behind you,
bloody hell, if you're stuck

for a light, they're like giant matches,
straight up. I'm not struck on white-

collar staff myself. I'm not saying
you don't do a hard day's work

but bloody hell, it must be boring
drinking tea and watching the clock.

Are you a doctor? I see
your briefcase against the wall.

Christ, I hope no-one's waiting for you,
clinging to their last breath.

Hey up we're off, about bloody time.

GET UP YOU LAZY BUGGER!
HAD A HARD DAY PAL?

Sleeping it off are you?
Christ, I hope you're not dead.

Arthur and The Rent Collector

I call him the rent man,
I don't know his name.

I see him in the park
sketching people and dogs

on scraps of paper and used envelopes.
Children flock to him, charmed

by his speed of hand and pencils
that smudge pictures to life.

He doesn't realise that to us,
his give-aways are like priceless works of art.

They'd be grand above his mantelpiece
or better still, framed, in one of them galleries

where people ooh and aah,
like the crowd in The Emperor's New Clothes.

Look at him in his rent collector suit
and long raincoat, like a right money man.

The Cripples

Children look up
at the war-wounded
as if to bombard them with questions.

But not all that we see are
home from the war:
the polio leg, scoliosis, the stroke.

'Don't stare,'
a black-eyed boy front left tells his sister.
Or perhaps not.

Perhaps he is about to lift her
so that like grown-ups
she can feast her eyes on a closer look.

The broken man in the middle,
deep in thought, opts out
of the pantomime and walks his dog

while the child, hand-out on the right
startles the double amputee
by asking for a turn on his trolley.

Shift

Going to Work, 1959

The only shadows you see around here
are the five o'clock ones on faces.

Shift workers up at the crack of
fried bacon on days, up in time for last orders

on nights. I don't need an alarm clock,
not with next door's squawking kids.

I never want kids; never want to be
a father, I'd rather bat for the other team

than turn out like my old man. He can
go to hell. All I wanted was a bit of fun,

she knew the score, where's the harm?
I might have told her she was special

and Christ, she was. But I never made
any promises: I never mentioned love.

A Protest March

Get out of the road, dogs!
They're coming, marching
but this lot aren't from
the factories, they're too
well dressed, too high
and mighty to carry banners.
They're obviously in ranks,
big knobs first. One or two
women add a token red
to the black and grey prism.
But why my street? Why
not take the scenic route
instead? Scenic my arse.
They just want us to see
power on the move. This
is no protest, more a march.
Not a sound from neighbours
as they stand still and watch.
The men bow their heads,
one man stands erect!
Silly buggers, it's politics
not a bloody funeral march.

A Doctor's Waiting Room

Ray said wearing a condom was
like chewing toffee with the wrapper on

so he didn't wear one.
He said you can't fall wrong

first time, especially standing up.
I always thought it would be

like in the movies: soft lights, music.
The queue for the flicks had stretched

the length of the lane.
I could taste the Brylcreem

as he leaned over to light a fag.
I felt in my handbag to see if

I had enough for both of us
as well as the bus fare home.

I read somewhere, we remember
things in a certain way, that memories

survive sleep, coma, cold and heat.
I remember coming out of the Odeon,

how he pulled me into a doorway
to escape the rain. I remember

his fingers, cold and wet, crawling
like caterpillars between my legs.

Waiting for the Shop To Open

She told me, 'You can't miss it,
just past Woolworths, opposite

the pork butchers, Blenkinsop's,
where we buy our savaloy dips.'

The last thing on my mind was
savaloy dips. All that warm

sausage and gravy in a bun.
I'd run a mile, throw up

if I got a whiff of one. I'd been
sick every morning all week.

I was about to turn for home when
I saw the sign above the Chemist's.

I'd never known it by another name,
everyone knew it as *Dirty Dick's*,

the man they claimed could cure
anything, from VD to verrucas.

Market Scene, Northern Town

The lidded stalls are laden with everything
from home-made cakes to hand-me-downs.

Just gone eight bells and the church clock
grinds to a tock. It must be Sunday,

women are wearing hats. They've
spilled out from early morning mass,

freshly blessed and raring to bag a bargain,
scudding across the cobbles, like shipyard workers

knocking off. One woman bends over to take
a closer look; holier than thou, she'll pinch the goods

between finger and thumb in gloves she has
worn in bed since that night on her honeymoon.

Note how 'the hats' keep their backs to the woman
in the shawl. Martha, mother, sister,

miracle worker; she can turn bones into broth.
Walk by The Dwellings tomorrow and you will know

her home: the polished letter box, sash windows,
open just enough to let you smell the pearl barley,

carrots, potatoes and onions, the stock bubbling
nicely in the pot; steam rising up like a prayer.

House on the Moor

Green hills surround the house
as if in a game of ring o' roses.

Air so still, mist creeps slowly
as in a recurring bad dream.

Only the lost and the lonely come here,
drawn by bleak familiarity, like a church

that lures the faithful to prayer.
And what do we ask for

if not the comfort of a kiss,
forgiveness and daily bread:

one night spent with a lover
in the depths of a warm double bed.

Putting Aunt Adeline On the Train

Head of a Woman in a Feathered Hat

I'd never tried cheese and pineapple
until I met Aunt Adeline;

never seen a real feather in a hat.
I thought perfume smelled of violets

and petticoats were flannelette.
Until I met Aunt Adeline

I'd never heard of South Africa,
anyone coming to visit came from Blyth.

But I learned so much in that fortnight,
so much about a different life.

As her train steamed away from the station
I asked my mother, 'Mam, what's *apartheid*?'

And Mam, like a ventriloquist and still waving,
'Fasten your coat, you look cold.' replied.

Nancy Drever

Flowers in a Window

She called herself the family star; wore a hat
while her sisters wore headscarves. A favourite

hat given to her by the doctor's wife, grateful
to Nancy for good housekeeping, the cast-off

worn like a trophy in every photograph.
She took to tartan after marrying George;

a skirt in black watch, bottle green cardigan
and *Plaisir D'Amour* that she dabbed

behind her ears on birthdays and Christmas.
She donkey-stoned her doorstep on Thursdays,

polished George on Wednesdays and if it wasn't
a good drying day, gave Mondays a dirty look.

The Funeral Party

No chapel, no footpath, no flowers.
Something doesn't sit right in this sad line-up.

They're all there, the knock-kneed women
and clown-feet men. The lass in the middle

looks side-eyed at the woman on the end:
Maybe she owes her money, maybe she stole her man.

She's keeping one hand in her pocket now,
keeping her hand on her ha'penny.

The strawberry blonde chap looks pasty,
like a solicitor, tormented by his client's ghost.

But what was the bloke far right thinking of,
to turn up late in boots and red tie?

He's obviously been told to face the other way;
in disgrace for his 'lack of respect'.

You'd take him for a naughty schoolboy
if it wasn't for the swell of his fly and his moustache.

After the Wedding

The dress will be wrapped in tissue paper
and returned to its cardboard box where

Lil keeps it, like a lover, under her bed.
Part-time dressmaker, full-time factory worker,

the dress is on loan to her best friend, the bride.
Lil's finished with waiting at the factory gates

long after clocking off; done with putting
her lipstick on in case 'Elvis' from the warehouse

asks her for a light. Lil, who still fancies herself
as a dancer and dreams of nights at the Tower

Ballroom: 'Slow, slow, quick quick, slow, Elvis!'
she sighs every night as she flings the bedclothes back.

But no hanging back at the wedding Do tonight:
Always the bridesmaid, she'll make sure the other two

don't win the cat fight when the bride tosses her bouquet
over her shoulder, like salt. The dress, though creased

and confetti'd with soot, will be scrubbed up
and boxed as if lying in state. Something old,

something new, something borrowed, something blue.
A kiss from a chimney sweep for good luck.

Head of a Young Man in a Cap

He looks posh even in his flat cap.
His mouth reminds me of a pen pal I had

when I was a girl. He was twenty-one,
I was too young so I sent him photos

of our Shirley instead. He sent me poems
in blue envelopes stamped, *Par Avion.*

I'd read them in bed and imagine him
looking into my eyes and whispering

Par Avion. I took on a different persona;
pretended to smoke and shrugged my shoulders.

He was happy for me to write in English
and sometimes he would do the same.

Letters from France fizzled out like a sparkler.
There were fireworks when my father found out.

He asked me, 'Who the hell's Serge?'
I pretended I hadn't heard. He asked me again

and threw the letters in the fire. I told him
he was no-one as under my breath I muttered, *Merde.*

A Letter from London

Piccadilly Circus, 1960

In many ways it is not so different from home,
bar the tourists and red buses. People criss-cross
in straight lines along the busy street as if
in formation dance teams or swirl around
a monument with the figure of a naked chap
perched on the top, a small, winged figure,
Eros, the God of Love. You do not expect
a famous London landmark to be coal black,
but there it is. I plan to paint one or two scenes
eventually and to visit my aunt, of course.
You must come with me next time. It would be
nice to have company. I could seek out a little hotel
and we could go to the ballet. We could
dine in fine restaurants, ride in black taxis!

You would like it here.

Sincerely,

Mother

The Bedroom, Pendlebury

While she sleeps, I paint.

In the early hours, fourteen plus
clocks to keep me company,

clocks and Bellini.

No-one else
is allowed to see her like this, bedridden,
longing still for a daughter

instead of this 'clumsy boy.'

I alone am allowed to nurse her,
spoon-feed her
the crumbs of the day.

In time, I shall paint the scene; capture
the emptiness when she is gone:

the dead white sheets
and the old blanket-box,
the solitary chair against the wall.

For now, a bloodshot portrait
as knuckles of coal fall to the hearth.

Two People

It's my long fingers that have kept us close,
so close we've mushroomed into almost the same shape.

Unlike all the other women in his life,
it was my small feet that first attracted him to me;

the novelty of never having to watch his step.
We could almost be ink blots, 'half human,

half animal' and difficult to know if I'm facing front.
Some say we're like a 'cartoon' couple

but we don't do too badly for two people
who've been through life's mill.

We may look odd against the white background
but at the end of the day we had the last laugh:

Grateful that the chemist's shop was closed that morning
and after all these years plus eleven grandchildren,

we're that devoted little couple, painted
on what might well have been a discarded cigar box.

Indigo Dreams Publishing
24 Forest Houses
Halwill
Beaworthy
Devon
EX21 5UU
www.indigodreams.co.uk